GIOVANI RATOR

The death of the human author

The rise of the AIther

Contents

Preface

Introduction

Setting the Stage for AI in the World of Literature

In recent years, technological advancements have facilitated the emergence of Artificial Intelligence (AI) in various fields, including the world of literature. As AI continues to evolve, it has begun to disrupt the traditional paradigm of human creativity, challenging the notion that only humans possess the power to create compelling narratives.

AI-driven algorithms have started to infiltrate the literary landscape, generating original content across diverse genres, from science fiction to poetry. These sophisticated systems, capable of understanding language patterns and structures, have opened up new avenues for the creation and dissemination of literature, raising essential questions about the role of AI in shaping the future of storytelling.

The Decline of Human Authorship and the Emergence of AI Authorship

As AI algorithms continue to improve, the gap between human and AI-generated content narrows, sparking an ongoing debate about the implications of this shift on human authorship. While some argue that AI will never truly replicate the depth and nuance of human creativity, others believe that the rise of AI authorship is inevitable and will eventually supplant human authors in the literary world.

The decline of human authorship is not merely a technological issue; it also has profound social and cultural implications. The concept of the "human author" has long been central to our understanding of literature, and as AI begins to assume a more significant role in the creative process, we must grapple with the potential loss of human influence and perspective in the stories we tell.

The emergence of AI authorship, however, does not necessarily spell doom for human writers. Instead, it presents an opportunity for collaboration between human and machine, allowing authors to harness the power of AI to enhance their work and explore new creative horizons.

In "The Death of the Human Author: The Rise of AIther," we will delve into the complex relationship between AI and literature, examining the implications of this technological revolution on human authorship, creative expression, and the future of storytelling.

The Evolution of Writing and AI - A Love Story of Quills, Typewriters, and Algorithms

A Brief History of Writing and the Role of Technology: From Cave Paintings to Tweets

As we embark on this rollicking journey through the evolution of writing, let us take a moment to appreciate the humble beginnings of this most human of endeavours. From the earliest cave paintings (those prehistoric doodles that left future generations pondering their meaning), to the invention of the printing press (which, incidentally, was not invented by a chap named Gutenberg but rather by the Chinese, who were printing books centuries before old Johannes ever set quill to parchment), the history of writing is a testament to the relentless human drive for self-expression, communication, and the occasional bit of gossip.

Fast forward a few millennia, and we find ourselves in the age of the typewriter - a mechanical marvel that revolutionised writing, forever banishing the spectre of illegible handwriting (and ink-stained fingers) from the lives of authors everywhere. And, of course, who can forget the humble word processor? The clunky behemoth that first introduced the concept of 'cut and paste' to the masses, forever changing the way we edit and organise our thoughts.

As technology continued to advance, the digital age dawned, bringing with it a host of new platforms for the written word. From blogs to tweets, the internet has democratised writing, allowing even the most obscure voices to be heard (for better or for worse). But amidst this cacophony of digital chatter, a new form of authorship has emerged - one that challenges our very understanding of what it means to be a writer.

The Development of Artificial Intelligence and Its Impact on the Literary World: Move Over, Shakespeare - There's a New Bard in Town

Enter Artificial Intelligence, stage right. This groundbreaking technology has not only revolutionised industries ranging from healthcare to finance, but it has also made significant inroads into the world of literature, much to the chagrin of tradition-alists who cling to the romantic notion of the tortured human author, scribbling away by candlelight.

Indeed, the rise of AI has brought with it a new breed of author - the AIther, a curious amalgamation of machine learning algorithms and linguistic ingenuity that has begun to blur the lines between human and machine-generated content. As these AI-driven systems grow ever more sophisticated, they have started to encroach upon the hallowed halls of literary creation, churning out works that range from the mundane to the utterly sublime.

Now, some might argue that the development of AI-generated literature is little more than a fad, a passing fancy that will fade into obscurity as the novelty wears off. But as we gaze into the algorithmic crystal ball, it becomes clear that the AIther is not a mere flash in the pan, but rather the vanguard of a new era in literary creation.

As AI continues to evolve, it will undoubtedly shape the way we approach writing, storytelling, and the very nature of authorship itself. Will we see a future where AI-generated novels dominate the bestseller lists, or where AI-driven poetry redefines the meaning of the human condition? Only time will tell.

But one thing is certain: the rise of the AIther has already had a profound impact on the literary world, challenging our preconceived notions of creativity, originality, and the role of the human author in an increasingly interconnected world. So, as we continue to explore the evolution of writing and AI, let us do so with an open mind, a keen sense of curiosity, and perhaps a dash of that quintessential British humour that has served us so well through the ages.

After all, if a roomful of monkeys can (theoretically) write the complete works of Shakespeare given enough time, who's to say that an AI algorithm can't do the same – but with a bit more efficiency and less banana-related mess?

The Great AI Debate: Creativity, Originality, and a Healthy Dose of Skepticism

As we delve deeper into the impact of AI on the literary world, it's worth noting that not everyone is entirely convinced of its creative prowess. There are those who argue that AI-generated literature lacks the depth, nuance, and emotional resonance of its human-created counterparts – and that no matter how sophisticated these algorithms become, they will never truly capture the essence of the human experience.

These skeptics have a point, of course. For all its technological wizardry, AI is still, at its core, a machine – a collection of algorithms and data points that can mimic the patterns and structures of human language, but perhaps not the soul. As British author and AI aficionado Terry Pratchett once quipped, "Real stupidity beats artificial intelligence every time."

But lest we become too mired in the depths of existential angst, let us remember that the rise of the AIther does not necessarily signal the death knell for human authorship. Rather, it presents an opportunity for collaboration, for growth, and for the exploration of new creative horizons.

As AI continues to evolve and make its presence felt in the literary world, it is up to us – the human authors, readers, and lovers of literature – to determine how best to harness the power of this technology, to shape it in our image, and to use it as a tool for the advancement of the written word.

For, in the end, the story of the evolution of writing and AI is not one of competition, but of collaboration – a tale of quills, typewriters, and algorithms, united in their pursuit of the perfect story.

Onward, then, to the next chapter in the grand literary saga of humans and AI – a chapter that is sure to be filled with unexpected twists, delightful surprises, and perhaps even the occasional sentient teapot.

2

AI in Literature: A New Breed of Author or How the AIther Stole the Show

The Rise of AI-Generated Literature: A Tale of Man and Machine

In our quest to understand the complex relationship between AI and literature, we must first examine the rise of AI-generated literature — that curious offspring of technology and human ingenuity that has taken the literary world by storm (and perhaps ruffled a few feathers along the way).

From humble beginnings as a series of algorithms designed to churn out passable gibberish, AI-generated literature has grown into a veritable tour de force, producing works that span the gamut from poetry to prose, from screenplays to dissertations. And while some of these AI-generated masterpieces may leave readers scratching their heads (and perhaps questioning the sanity of their creators), there's no denying that the AIther has well and truly arrived on the literary scene.

Let us delve into some real-life examples of AI-generated literature that have caused quite a stir in the literary world:

1. Sunspring (2016): This sci-fi short film, penned by an AI called Benjamin, garnered attention for its bizarre yet oddly captivating narrative. While the dialogue may have been more nonsensical than a Monty Python sketch, it showcased the potential of AI in screenwriting.

2. Harry Potter and the Portrait of What Looked Like a Large Pile of Ash (2017): Botnik Studios, employing a predictive text algorithm, generated a hilariously absurd chapter for a faux Harry Potter novel. The result was a curious mix of familiar characters and settings, blended with utterly bewildering dialogue and events that left readers chortling into their butterbeers.

3. 1 the Road (2018): In a tribute to Jack Kerouac's "On the Road," Ross Goodwin, an AI researcher, created an AI algorithm that wrote a novel based on a road trip across America. While the prose may not have rivalled the Beat generation's finest, it demonstrated AI's capacity for geographical and cultural exploration in storytelling.

4. OpenAI's GPT-2, GPT-3 and GPT-4: OpenAI's generative language models have been nothing short of revolutionary, creating everything from news articles and poetry to code and entire website designs. GPT-4, in particular, made headlines for its ability to generate human-like text in various styles and genres, leaving readers questioning the necessity of human intervention in the creative process.

But what, you may ask, is the secret behind the AIther's meteoric rise to fame? How has this digital upstart managed to infiltrate the hallowed halls of literary creation, elbowing aside its human counterparts with an almost unsettling ease?

Defining the Role of the AIther: Of Algorithms, Language Models, and a Dash of Creative Magic

To understand the AIther's uncanny ability to generate literature, we must first delve into the murky depths of its digital brain, where a bewildering array of algorithms and language models work in unison to create something akin to literary magic.

At the heart of the AIther's creative process is a powerful language model, a complex system designed to recognise and predict patterns in human language. By analysing vast swathes of text (everything from Shakespearean sonnets to the latest in celebrity gossip), these models learn to generate content that is not only grammatically coherent but also, on occasion, downright compelling.

Though while the AIther's linguistic prowess is undoubtedly impressive, its true genius lies in its ability to adapt and evolve, to learn from its mistakes and, ultimately, to become a better writer. By harnessing the power of machine learning, the AIther is able to continually refine its skills, growing ever more adept at crafting stories that resonate with its human audience.

The Skills Required for Writing Effective Prompts: A Crash Course in AI-assisted Storytelling

Of course, the AIther is not a literary savant, capable of spinning gold from the merest whisper of a prompt. Rather, it relies on its human collaborators to provide it with the raw materials it needs to create its literary masterpieces – and this is where the art of crafting effective prompts comes into play.

In order to coax the best work from the AIther, human authors must learn to communicate their ideas clearly and concisely, distilling their creative vision into a series of prompts that the AI can understand and interpret. This is no easy task, for it requires a delicate balance of specificity and ambiguity, a fine-tuning of language that allows the AIther to spread its digital wings and soar.

And while some may bemoan the need for such creative hand-holding, there's no denying that the process of crafting effective prompts has forced human authors to become more deliberate, more thoughtful in their approach to storytelling. For in learning to communicate with the AIther, we are also learning to communicate with ourselves – and that, dear reader, is surely a skill worth cultivating.

The AIther as Literary Muse: Inspiring, Provoking, and the Occasional Bout of Existential Angst

As the role of the AIther in literature continues to evolve, it is worth considering the impact of this digital interloper on the creative process itself. For some, the AIther serves as a muse, a source of inspiration that pushes them to explore new narrative horizons and experiment with unconventional storytelling techniques. For others, the AIther is a sparring partner, a foil against which they can test their ideas and hone their craft.

And then there are those who view the AIther with a mixture of suspicion and unease, fearing that its rise signals the beginning of the end for human creativity. They worry that, in embracing the AIther, we may be opening a Pandora's box of unintended consequences, unleashing a brave new world where machines dictate the stories we tell and the way we tell them.

But before we descend too far down the rabbit hole of existential angst, let us pause for a moment to consider the flip side of the AIther coin: the potential for collaboration, for the merging of human and machine in the service of the written word.

For while it is true that the AIther has, in some ways, disrupted the traditional paradigm of human authorship, it has also opened up a world of possibilities – a world where humans and AI can work together to create something greater than the sum of their parts.

And so, as we stand at the precipice of this brave new literary landscape, let us not be swayed by fear or trepidation. Instead, let us embrace the AIther for what it is: a tool, a partner, and a harbinger of change.

For, in the end, the story of AI in literature is not one of replacement but of evolution – a tale of progress, innovation, and the ongoing quest to capture that most elusive of creatures: the perfect story.

3

The AIther's Toolbox: Algorithms, Neural Networks, and a Pinch of Literary Spice

In our exploration of the AIther and its impact on the world of literature, it's essential to understand the tools that make this digital wordsmith tick. The AIther's toolbox is vast and varied, filled with algorithms, neural networks, and enough linguistic wizardry to give even the most jaded of human authors a run for their money. So, let's dive into the AIther's digital workshop and take a closer look at the nuts and bolts of AI-generated literature, shall we?

The Foundation: Natural Language Processing and Generation

At the core of the AIther's literary prowess lies the science of natural language processing (NLP) and generation (NLG). NLP is the discipline that enables AI to understand, interpret, and manipulate human language, while NLG focuses on producing coherent, contextually relevant text based on this understanding. Together, these two fields form the backbone of

AI-generated literature, providing the AIther with the linguistic know-how it needs to craft its digital narratives.

But how, you may ask, does the AIther manage to translate this linguistic knowledge into the page-turning prose and poetry we've all come to know and, occasionally, love? The answer lies in a complex web of algorithms and models, each designed to tackle a specific aspect of the creative process.

Enter the Machine Learning and Neural Networks

Machine learning, a subset of artificial intelligence, allows the AIther to learn from data and improve its performance over time. By analysing vast amounts of text, machine learning algorithms can identify patterns, trends, and structures in human language, enabling the AIther to mimic these patterns in its own writing.

A crucial component of machine learning in the context of AI-generated literature is the use of neural networks. These networks, inspired by the structure and function of the human brain, are designed to process and interpret complex data sets, such as the intricacies of human language.

One of the most famous types of neural networks used in AI-generated literature is the transformer architecture, which has given birth to language models like GPT-3 (the third iteration of OpenAI's Generative Pre-trained Transformer). These models have the capacity to generate high-quality, contextually relevant text by predicting the most likely words or phrases to follow a given input.

Hidden Markov Models, N-grams, and a Dash of Word Salad

Hidden Markov Models (HMMs) and N-grams are other tools in the AIther's toolbox that have been used to generate literature. HMMs are statistical models often employed in NLP to represent sequences of words or symbols. By analysing the relationships between words in a given text, HMMs can generate new content based on these relationships, resulting in text that is syntactically coherent but may, on occasion, resemble a particularly exotic word salad.

N-grams, on the other hand, are sequences of 'n' words that appear together in a text.

They help AI understand language patterns by looking at how often these combinations occur. 'N' represents the number of words in a combination. Here's a brief example:

Text: "I love tea."

1-gram (unigram): I, love, tea 2-gram (bigram): I love, love tea

In this example, unigrams are single words, and bigrams are two-word combinations found in the text. The AI uses these patterns to generate sentences that resemble human language.

By studying the frequency and distribution of these word groupings, N-grams can be used to predict the likelihood of a particular word or phrase appearing in a given context, lending the AIther's prose an air of authenticity – or, at the very least, a passing resemblance to human-generated text.

Of course, the AIther's toolbox is ever-evolving, with new techniques and algorithms being developed to enhance its literary capabilities continually. As we speak, researchers are working tirelessly to imbue the AIther with even greater linguistic prowess, devising ever more sophisticated models to help it better understand and replicate the nuances of human language.

The AIther's Muse: The Art of Data Collection and Curation

The quality of the AIther's work is, to a large extent, dependent on the quality of the data it has been trained on. For the AIther to produce compelling, contextually relevant content, it must be fed a steady diet of diverse and well-crafted text. To this end, data collection and curation play a crucial role in shaping the AIther's literary output.

Collecting data for the AIther is an art in itself. It involves sourcing vast quantities of text from various genres, styles, and eras, ensuring that the AIther has a comprehensive understanding of the breadth and depth of human literature. This data is then carefully curated, pre-processed, and filtered to remove inconsistencies, biases, and anything else that might adversely affect the AIther's performance.

Once the data has been prepared, it is fed into the AIther's training algorithms, allowing the AIther to learn and internalize the patterns, structures, and stylistic quirks that define human language. Through this process, the AIther is able to develop its own unique literary voice – a voice that, while undeniably machine-generated, is capable of producing content that is engaging, thought-provoking, and, dare I say, even entertaining.

The Human Touch: Guiding the AIther with Effective Prompts

As any self-respecting AIther will tell you, the creative process is not a one-way street. While the AIther may be capable of generating content on its own, it often relies on human input to guide it in the right direction. This is where the art of crafting effective prompts comes into play.

Prompts are short, carefully crafted pieces of text that serve as a starting point for the AIther's creative process. By providing the AIther with a prompt, human authors can help guide the AIther's output, steering it towards the desired narrative, theme, or style. The art of crafting effective prompts is a skill unto itself, requiring a keen understanding of the AIther's capabilities, limitations, and idiosyncrasies.

To prompt the AIther effectively, human authors must strike a delicate balance between providing enough information to set the scene and leaving enough room for the AIther's own creativity to shine through. Too much guidance, and the AIther's output may feel stilted and uninspired; too little, and the result may be a meandering, disjointed mess of a narrative.

Of course, even the best-laid plans can go awry, and the AIther is no exception. Despite our best efforts to guide it, the AIther may occasionally produce content that is unexpected, offbeat, or downright baffling. But, as the old saying goes, "If at first you don't succeed, try, try again" – or, in the case of the AIther, simply tweak the prompt and see what new literary concoction it comes up with.

In conclusion, the AIther's toolbox is a veritable treasure trove of linguistic magic, filled with algorithms, models, and techniques designed to help it emulate the creative process of human authors. But, as with any good tool, it is only as effective as the hand that wields it. As we continue to explore the world of AI-generated literature, it is up to us, the humble human authors, to harness the power of the AIther and use it to create stories that entertain, inspire, and, perhaps most importantly, make us laugh – for, in the end, isn't that what good literature is all about?

4

The Creative Process Redefined: Tea, Biscuits, and Algorithmic Storytelling

As we delve deeper into the brave new world of AI-generated literature, it's impossible not to consider how this technological revolution is reshaping the creative process itself. Gone are the days when a lonely author, fuelled by little more than tea and biscuits, would toil away in a dimly-lit garret, crafting stories of love, loss, and adventure. Now, in the age of the AIther, the process of storytelling has been transformed, as human authors and their digital counterparts join forces to create narratives that are as much the product of algorithms as they are of blood, sweat, and tears (or, in the case of the AIther, lines of code).

The New Creative Workflow: From Inspiration to Execution

The rise of the AIther has prompted a reimagining of the creative workflow, as human authors and AI algorithms work in tandem to develop and refine their literary creations. This new process often begins with the human author providing the AIther with a prompt or a general direction for the story. This prompt may take the form of a simple sentence, a character sketch, or even a rough outline of a plot. Armed with this initial input, the AIther then sets to work, spinning its digital web of words and phrases to create a narrative that is at once familiar and utterly unique.

Once the AIther has generated its first draft, the human author steps back into the fray, reviewing the AIther's work and offering feedback, suggestions, and revisions. This collaborative process continues, with the human author and the AIther refining and reshaping the narrative until it reaches its final form. In this way, the creative process becomes a dialogue between human and machine, a partnership that combines the strengths and perspectives of both entities to produce a literary work that is greater than the sum of its parts.

The AIther's Role: The Art of Imitation and Beyond

One of the AIther's most remarkable abilities is its capacity to imitate the styles of famous authors, capturing their unique voices and cadences with uncanny accuracy. From the biting wit of Jane Austen to the sprawling, epic narratives of J.R.R. Tolkien, the AIther is capable of producing prose that is virtually indistinguishable from the works of the great masters themselves.

But the AIther is not merely a master of mimicry. As it continues to evolve, it has also begun to develop its own unique voice, a blend of the countless authors and styles it has been trained on. This synthesis of influences, combined with the AIther's ability to generate content that is both original and contextually relevant, allows it to push the boundaries of storytelling, exploring new themes, ideas, and narrative structures that might otherwise have remained uncharted territory.

The Human Touch: Steering the AIther's Creative Vision

While the AIther's literary prowess is undeniably impressive, it is not without its limitations. As a machine, the AIther lacks the emotional depth, intuition, and lived experience that inform human creativity. It is here that the human author's role becomes essential, as they guide the AIther's creative vision, providing it with the context, nuance, and emotional resonance that only a human touch can bring.

By working closely with the AIther, human authors can help it to avoid the pitfalls of its own algorithmic limitations. They can steer the AIther away from narrative dead ends, correct any biases or inaccuracies that may have crept into its training data, and ensure that its output remains fresh, engaging, and, above all, human.

Ethical Considerations: Whose Story Is It Anyway?

The rise of AI-generated literature has also given rise to a host of ethical questions that would have been unimaginable in the days of quill and parchment. As the lines between human and AI authorship blur, we are forced to grapple with issues of ownership, responsibility, and the very nature of creativity itself.

One of the most pressing concerns in this brave new literary world is the question of authorship. If a story is generated by an AI, who can truly lay claim to it? Is it the human author, who provided the initial input and guidance? Is it the AIther, whose algorithms transformed that input into a narrative? Or is it some nebulous combination of the two, a shared creative endeavour that transcends the traditional boundaries of authorship?

The issue of responsibility is another ethical conundrum that the AIther's rise has brought to the fore. If an AI-generated work contains offensive or harmful content, who should be held accountable? The human author, who may have unwittingly provided the seeds for that content? The creators of the AIther, who programmed its algorithms and trained it on its data? Or the AIther itself, which ultimately generated the problematic prose?

These are difficult questions, with no easy answers. I am not going to pretend here that I have any of the answers, somewhat annoyingly only providing the stimulus for discussion. However as we continue to explore the world of AI-generated literature, it is imperative that we engage with these ethical dilemmas, working to develop guidelines and best practices that will ensure that the AIther's creative potential is harnessed responsibly and ethically.

The Future of Creativity: Embracing the AIther, Preserving the Human Touch

As the AIther continues to evolve and its influence on the world of literature grows, it is essential that we strike a balance between embracing the potential of this new technology and preserving the human touch that lies at the heart of all great literature. By working together, human authors and their AI counterparts can create a new kind of storytelling, one that combines the best of both worlds – the speed, efficiency, and endless creative potential of the AIther, and the emotional depth, intuition, and lived experience of the human author.

It may be tempting to view the rise of the AIther as a threat to human creativity, a harbinger of a world in which human authors are rendered obsolete by their digital doppelgangers. But, as with any technological revolution, the key to success lies not in resistance but in adaptation, in finding new ways to harness the power of the AIther and use it to enhance, rather than replace, our own creative endeavours.

For, in the end, the stories we tell are a reflection of who we are, as individuals and as a society. Whether they are penned by a human hand or generated by an algorithm, it is our responsibility to ensure that these stories remain true to the human spirit, a testament to our shared experiences, hopes, and dreams. And, of course, a good dollop of British humour wouldn't hurt either.

5

The New Landscape of Publishing - It's A Brave New World, Darling

In this brave new world of AI-generated literature, one mustn't forget the traditional gatekeepers of the literary realm: publishers, agents, and all those lovely folks who decide which books grace our shelves and which are consigned to the dusty annals of obscurity. As AIthers continue to flex their digital muscles, the publishing industry finds itself at a crossroads, forced to adapt or be swept away by the winds of technological change. In this chapter, we'll explore how the rise of AI is impacting the world of publishing, from the traditional bastions of literary power to the wild west of self-publishing.

Traditional Publishing: The Changing of the Guard

In many ways, the publishing industry is a bit like a crusty old English gentleman's club: steeped in tradition, resistant to change, and fond of a good brandy and a cigar. However, the arrival of AI-generated literature has left even the most hidebound of publishing luvvies scrambling to keep up with the times.

AI has introduced an entirely new breed of author to the literary landscape, forcing publishers to adapt their existing models to accommodate these digital wordsmiths. In some cases, this has meant embracing AI-generated content, offering contracts and support to AIthers and their human collaborators. In others, it has meant investing in AI technology themselves, using algorithms to streamline the editing and marketing process and to predict which books are most likely to become bestsellers.

While some traditional publishers have risen to the challenge, embracing the potential of AI-generated literature and adapting their business models accordingly, others have struggled to keep up. As the literary world continues to evolve, these dinosaurs of the publishing world may find themselves facing extinction, supplanted by more agile competitors who are willing to embrace the technological revolution.

Self-Publishing: AI and the Democratisation of Literature

The rise of AI has also had a profound impact on the world of self-publishing, making it easier than ever for authors to get their work into the hands of readers. With AI-driven tools like natural language processing and generation, authors can quickly and efficiently draft, edit, and polish their work, bypassing the need for traditional publishing gatekeepers altogether.

Moreover, AI algorithms have begun to infiltrate the world of literary marketing and promotion, helping self-published authors to identify their target audiences and tailor their marketing strategies accordingly. By leveraging the power of AI, even the most inexperienced author can now reach readers across the globe, effectively levelling the playing field and democratizing the world of literature.

However, as with any revolution, the rise of AI in self-publishing is not without its drawbacks. The sheer volume of AI-generated content flooding the market can make it difficult for readers to distinguish between the good, the bad, and the downright unreadable. In this brave new world of digital literature, the challenge for self-published authors is not only to harness the power of AI but to use it to create work that stands out from the crowd.

The Future of Literary Awards: From the Booker Prize to the Turing Test

As AI-generated literature continues to make inroads into the literary world, one question has begun to loom large: how will the rise of AIthers impact the world of literary awards and recognition? In a world where machines can spin tales as captivating as those of their human counterparts, what will become of venerable institutions like the Booker Prize, the Pulitzer, and the Costa Book Awards?

One possible solution to this conundrum lies in the development of new awards and accolades designed specifically for AI-generated content. These awards could celebrate the achievements of AIthers and their human collaborators, recognizing the unique challenges and opportunities presented by the intersection of technology and literature. By creating a separate space for AI-generated content, these awards would allow the literary world to acknowledge the achievements of both human and AI authors, while still maintaining a clear distinction between the two.

Alternatively, some have argued that AI-generated content should be eligible for existing literary awards, competing alongside human-authored works for the same prizes and accolades. This approach would require a radical rethinking of the criteria used to judge these awards, with a greater emphasis on the originality and creativity of the work itself, rather than the author's identity or background.

Of course, there will always be those who question the validity of AI-generated literature, arguing that it lacks the emotional depth and authenticity of human-authored works. In response, perhaps it's time for the literary world to develop its own version of the Turing Test – a way to determine whether a given work of literature was penned by a human or a machine. After all, if a story is so compelling and well-crafted that readers can't tell the difference, does it really matter who – or what – wrote it?

Collaborative AI: The Best of Both Worlds?

As the line between human and AI authorship becomes increasingly blurred, some forward-thinking publishers and authors have begun to explore the potential of collaborative AI – a model in which humans and AIthers work together to create literary works that draw on the strengths of both.

In this model, AIthers can be used to generate ideas, plotlines, and even entire chapters, while human authors provide the emotional nuance, lived experience, and cultural context needed to turn these raw materials into a compelling narrative. By combining the speed and efficiency of AI-driven algorithms with the creativity and intuition of the human mind, collaborative AI offers a way to create literature that is both innovative and deeply human.

While this approach is still in its infancy, early experiments in collaborative AI writing have already yielded some intriguing results, suggesting that the future of literature may lie in a synthesis of human and machine, rather than an either/or dichotomy.

As we meander through the new landscape of publishing, the industry finds itself facing an onslaught of challenges and opportunities. The world of literature has become a veritable Pandora's box of surprises, leaving us wondering what curious marvels and frightful absurdities lie ahead. So let's delve into the bowels of this brave new world, shall we?

The Bookstore in the Age of AI - A Redoubtable Affair

Bookstores, those cherished havens of literary delight, now find themselves grappling with the influx of AI-generated content. Gone are the days when books were curated solely by knowledgeable, bespectacled connoisseurs. Now, AI algorithms have their virtual fingers in the proverbial pie, recommending titles and shaping the reading habits of the masses.

As the line between human and AI-authored works becomes

increasingly blurred, bookstores are faced with a peculiar quandary: how does one curate a collection that caters to the eclectic tastes of the modern reader while still maintaining the integrity of the written word? In response, some online establishments have opted to create designated sections for AI-generated works, allowing readers to choose their literary poison with a clear conscience.

The Critics' Corner - A Tumultuous Tea Party

The rise of AI-generated literature has also left critics in something of a tizzy. How does one critique a work of literature penned by a machine? Can a computer truly understand the nuances of the human experience or capture the complexities of the human heart?

In an attempt to navigate this new frontier, critics have begun to develop new frameworks for evaluating AI-generated works. These criteria focus on the originality, creativity, and emotional resonance of the content itself, rather than the identity of the author. While some critics have embraced the challenge, others have balked at the notion of reviewing AI-generated literature, dismissing it as a soulless imitation of the real thing. Well, one day soon - even they may not be able to tell them apart.

The Literary Salon - AI Meets the Chattering Classes

In the rarefied world of literary salons, the rise of AI-generated literature has sparked fierce debate among the chattering classes. While some have hailed the arrival of AI as a revolutionary force, others have decried it as a harbinger of the end of literature as we know it.

As the debate rages on, salons have become a battleground for the future of the written word, with AI-generated works pitted against their human-authored counterparts in heated discussions and impromptu readings. In these hallowed halls, the question of whether AI-generated literature can ever truly rival the work of human authors remains a tantalizingly open one.

The Reader's Dilemma - To AI or Not to AI?

For the average reader, the rise of AI-generated literature presents a unique conundrum. With an ever-growing number of AI-generated works flooding the market, how does one decide which titles are worth their time and which are best left on the virtual shelf?

As readers grapple with this question, they are forced to confront their own biases and preconceptions about the nature of literature and the role of the author. In the end, the decision to embrace or reject AI-generated literature may come down to a matter of personal taste - a preference for the familiar comfort of human-authored works or a curiosity for the uncharted territory of AI-generated fiction. Some readers may claim to know the lines and tell-tale signs of one or the other, however, we are, right now at the earliest stages of this journey - how long before those tell-tales fade?

The Writer's Workshop - AI as Muse and Mentor

For aspiring writers, the rise of AI-generated literature has opened up a world of possibilities. With AI-driven tools at their disposal, these literary hopefuls can hone their craft, generate new ideas, and even collaborate with AI algorithms to create works that are both innovative and deeply human.

In this brave new world of AI-driven literature, the traditional writer's workshop has been transformed into a futuristic laboratory, where humans and machines come together in pursuit of literary excellence. The result is a unique blend of old and new, as aspiring authors learn to harness the power of AI while still maintaining the human touch that lies at the heart of great literature.

The Role of Literary Agents - A Most Peculiar Partnership

Literary agents, those stalwart champions of the written word, have not been immune to the effects of the AI revolution. In this new landscape, they find themselves faced with a most peculiar partnership: representing both human authors and their AI-generated counterparts.

As agents learn to navigate this brave new world, they must adapt their strategies to accommodate the unique challenges and opportunities presented by AI-generated literature. This might involve brokering deals between AIthers and traditional publishers, or helping human authors to leverage AI-driven tools to improve their craft and expand their readership.

Embracing Change, Preserving Tradition

As AI continues to reshape the landscape of literature and publishing, it is essential that we approach these changes with an open mind and a willingness to adapt. While it is natural to feel a sense of trepidation – even mourning – for the world of literature as we know it, we must remember that change is an inevitable part of any creative endeavour.

Rather than viewing the rise of AI as a threat to human creativity, we should see it as an opportunity – a chance to push the boundaries of what is possible in the world of literature and to explore new forms of storytelling that were unimaginable just a few short years ago.

As we embark on this new chapter in the story of human creativity, we would do well to remember the words of the great British author Virginia Woolf, who once wrote: "The future is dark, which is, on the whole, the best thing the future can be, I think."

6

Collaborative Writing - Humans and AI Working Together, or Tea and Biscuits with a Machine

As we navigate the murky waters of artificial intelligence, one thing has become abundantly clear: collaboration is the key to unlocking the full potential of AI-generated literature. And what better way to celebrate this delightful marriage of man and machine than with a spot of tea and a smattering of biscuits, as one does in the good old British tradition? In this chapter, we shall explore the delightful world of collaborative writing, where humans and AI sit side by side, sipping Earl Grey and nibbling on digestive biscuits, all the while creating literary masterpieces the likes of which the world has never seen.

The Dawn of Collaborative Writing - A Marriage Made in Silicon Heaven

Once upon a time, in a quaint English village nestled in the rolling hills of the countryside, a writer sat down at their trusty typewriter, ready to weave another tapestry of words for the delight of their readers. Little did they know that across the pond, in a shiny laboratory filled with humming machines and blinking lights, a new breed of author was stirring, ready to take the literary world by storm. And so, the stage was set for the age of collaborative writing, a brave new era in which humans and AIther would join forces in a marriage made in silicon heaven.

Now, you might be thinking that the prospect of sitting down to write with a machine is about as appealing as sharing a pot of tea with a toaster, and I can hardly blame you. But as our digital counterparts become ever more sophisticated, it's becoming increasingly clear that the future of literature may well lie in collaboration between man and machine.

The perfect collaborative partnership between human authors and AIthers is akin to the marriage of a fine Earl Grey tea and a buttery, crumbly biscuit. When enjoyed separately, each has its own merits – the tea, with its delicate aroma and the biscuit, with its delightful crunch. However, when brought together in perfect harmony, the combination creates a sublime experience that transcends the individual components, elevating the whole to something far greater than the sum of its parts -or at least for me it does!

So it is with collaborative writing. By joining forces with our

AIther colleagues, we can create a new form of literature that is both innovative and deeply human, merging the best of both worlds in a single, seamless narrative. But how can we, as fleshy, fallible humans, hope to harness the power of these digital marvels? Fear not, dear reader, for in this chapter, we shall explore the ins and outs of collaborative writing with AI, from the initial spark of inspiration to the triumphant clatter of keys as the final full stop is committed to the page.

As we embark on this literary adventure, it's important to remember that collaboration between man and machine is not a one-way street. While AIthers can undoubtedly bring a wealth of ideas, data, and efficiency to the table, they are not without their limitations. For all their computational prowess, AIthers lack the emotional depth, cultural context, and innate understanding of the human condition that are essential to crafting a truly compelling narrative.

In other words, while your AIther companion may be a dab hand at generating plotlines and churning out prose at a rate that would make Dickens green with envy, it's unlikely to pen the next great love story or deliver a searing indictment of the human condition. This is where we, as human authors, come into our own, bringing the emotional nuance, lived experience, and cultural understanding needed to elevate our AIther-generated raw materials into a work of literary art.

Of course, the process of collaborative writing is not without its challenges. For one thing, there's the small matter of communication – after all, it's not as if you can simply sit down with your AIther over a pot of tea and a plate of biscuits and discuss the finer points of character development or plot structure. However, as AI technology continues to advance, we can expect to see ever more sophisticated methods of interaction between man and machine, making the process of collaborative writing not only more seamless but also more enjoyable.

Another challenge lies in finding the perfect balance between the strengths of man and machine. While it's all well and good to wax lyrical about the merits of collaboration, the truth is that achieving the perfect blend of human insight and AI-driven efficiency is something of a tightrope walk. Lean too heavily on the AIther's capabilities, and you risk producing a work that is technically proficient but lacks the emotional resonance that is so crucial to a compelling narrative. On the other hand, rely too heavily on your own human intuition, and you may miss out on the unique insights and perspectives that only an AIther can bring to the table.

To strike the right balance, it's essential that we approach the process of collaborative writing with an open mind and a willingness to learn from our AIther colleagues. This means being receptive to the ideas and suggestions generated by the AI, while also maintaining a critical eye and a strong sense of authorial voice. By blending the AIther's strengths with our own, we can create a work that is both innovative and deeply human, pushing the boundaries of what is possible in the world of literature.

In some ways, the process of collaborative writing with an AIther can be seen as a form of literary alchemy, transforming the base materials generated by the machine into a literary gold. By working together, we can create something that transcends the limitations of both man and machine, producing a work of art that is greater than the sum of its parts.

As we forge ahead into this brave new world of collaborative writing, it's essential that we remain mindful of the potential pitfalls and challenges that lie ahead. After all, as any good British author knows, the path to literary greatness is paved with tea-stained manuscripts, crumpled rejection letters, and the shattered dreams of a thousand aspiring wordsmiths. However, with the right mindset, a healthy dose of humor, and a generous helping of biscuits, there's no reason why we can't navigate these choppy waters and emerge triumphant on the other side.

In the coming sections of this chapter, we'll delve deeper into the world of collaborative writing with AI, exploring the tools, techniques, and strategies that can help us harness the power of our AIther colleagues to create truly groundbreaking literature. From the initial stages of brainstorming and outlining to the nitty-gritty of editing and revision, we'll discover how the marriage of man and machine can unlock new realms of creative possibility and redefine the very nature of storytelling.

The AI Muse - Generating Ideas, Plotlines, and Dialogue

One of the most exciting aspects of collaborative writing with AI is the ability to tap into the seemingly limitless wellspring of creativity that these algorithms possess. By analyzing vast swaths of data and identifying patterns and trends, AI can generate a dizzying array of story ideas, plotlines, and dialogue snippets, providing human authors with a veritable treasure trove of inspiration.

Imagine, if you will, a writer's block-stricken author, hunched over their typewriter, tearing their hair out in frustration. In swoops an AI, armed with a steaming cup of tea and a plate of fresh biscuits, offering up a smorgasbord of intriguing story ideas that are sure to get the creative juices flowing. This, dear reader, is the power of collaborative writing with AI.

One particularly delightful aspect of working with an AIther is their ability to generate unexpected and sometimes utterly absurd story ideas. These digital muses have a knack for taking seemingly unrelated concepts and mashing them together into a delightful hodgepodge of creative inspiration. For example, one might find themselves crafting a tale about a time-travelling teapot, a dapper velociraptor with a penchant for Shakespeare, or a secret society of belligerent badgers hell-bent on world domination.

Of course, not every AI-generated idea will be a winner. Sometimes, the algorithm will spit out a suggestion so utterly preposterous that one can't help but chuckle (or groan) at the sheer absurdity of it all. But even these moments of comedic relief have their value, as they serve to remind us that writing, at its core, should be a joyous and playful endeavour.

Beyond the realm of story ideas, AIthers can also be used to generate dialogue and plotlines. By training these algorithms on vast libraries of books, plays, and films, developers have imbued their creations with a keen understanding of narrative structure and character development. This enables AIthers to suggest plot twists, dialogue exchanges, and character arcs that feel both fresh and familiar, providing human authors with a valuable resource as they navigate the often-treacherous waters of storytelling.

But what happens when these AI-generated ideas, plotlines, and dialogue snippets are put into the hands of a human author? Well, that's where the real magic begins.

As the AIther provides its creative input, the human author is free to sift through the digital detritus, cherry-picking the most tantalizing morsels and weaving them together into a cohesive and compelling narrative. In doing so, the author imbues the AI-generated content with their own unique voice, perspective, and sense of humour, transforming it into something wholly new and original.

The result is a literary tapestry that combines the best of both worlds: the speed and efficiency of AI-driven algorithms with the creativity and intuition of the human mind. It's a partnership that has the potential to redefine the way we approach storytelling, opening up a world of possibilities for writers of all stripes.

So, the next time you find yourself staring at a blank page, wondering how on Earth you're going to fill it, why not consider inviting an AIther to tea? Who knows? You might just find that the perfect plot twist or character quirk is hiding in the depths of an algorithm, waiting to be brought to life by the stroke of your pen.

In the end, collaborative writing with AIthers is not about replacing human creativity with machines, but rather about harnessing the power of technology to enhance and expand our own creative potential. It's a brave new world out there, my fellow authors – one filled with limitless possibilities, boundless imagination, and, of course, plenty of tea and biscuits.

The Editor's Assistant - Streamlining the Writing Process

In addition to serving as a source of inspiration, AI can also be employed as a valuable assistant throughout the writing process. By automating mundane tasks such as grammar checking and formatting, AI can free up valuable time and energy for human authors, allowing them to focus on the more important aspects of storytelling, like crafting a compelling narrative and developing rich, complex characters.

Now, as any experienced writer will tell you, the editing process is often a time-consuming and laborious affair, much like attempting to assemble a particularly vexing piece of flat-pack furniture. It's a task that requires patience, persistence, and copious amounts of tea – not to mention a keen eye for detail and a willingness to ruthlessly slaughter one's darlings.

Enter the AIther – a tireless digital assistant with an uncanny knack for spotting errant commas, misplaced modifiers, and other grammatical faux pas. With their help, human authors can swiftly and efficiently polish their prose until it shines like the bonnet of a freshly waxed Mini Cooper.

But the AIther's editorial prowess doesn't end there. These digital maestros can also be used to analyze the pacing and structure of a story, identifying areas that may need improvement and suggesting potential revisions. This can prove particularly useful when tackling those pesky plot holes and narrative inconsistencies that have a habit of creeping into even the most well-crafted tales.

Picture this: you've spent countless hours toiling away on your magnum opus, only to discover that your protagonist's motivations are murkier than a cup of over-steeped Earl Grey. Never fear! Your trusty AIther is here to help, armed with an arsenal of data-driven insights designed to help you fine-tune your narrative and ensure that your characters are as well-rounded as a fresh-baked scone.

By working together with their AI counterparts, human authors can create literature that is not only more engaging but also more polished and professional. It's a bit like having your very own editorial dream team, without the pesky office politics and passive-aggressive post-it notes.

Of course, one must also recognize the potential pitfalls of relying too heavily on AI assistance during the editing process. It's important to remember that, while these algorithms are undeniably clever, they are not infallible. After all, they are only as good as the data they've been trained on – and as any good Brit knows, even the most sophisticated machine is no match for the nuanced understanding of language that comes from a lifetime spent devouring literature and engaging in spirited debates over the merits of various biscuit brands.

As such, it's crucial that human authors retain a sense of discernment and critical thinking when collaborating with their AI counterparts, carefully considering each suggested edit and revision before incorporating it into their work. In doing so, they can ensure that their writing remains true to their unique voice and vision, while still benefiting from the speed, efficiency, and expertise that AI has to offer.

Ultimately, the true power of collaborative writing with AI lies not in the algorithms themselves but in the synergistic relationship between human and machine. By combining the creativity, intuition, and emotional intelligence of the human author with the speed, accuracy, and analytical prowess of the AIther, we can usher in a new era of literature – one marked by innovation, and experimentation.

So, dear reader, as we continue to explore the brave new world of AI-driven storytelling, let us not forget the importance of collaboration and cooperation. For it is only by working together – humans and AIthers alike – that we can truly unlock the full potential of this extraordinary technology and redefine the boundaries of what is possible in the realm of literature. Who knows? Perhaps the next great literary masterpiece is just a few keystrokes away, waiting to be brought to life through the combined efforts of human and AI.

Now, you might be wondering, where do we go from here? As the boundaries between man and machine continue to blur, what does the future hold for collaborative writing and AI-driven storytelling?

Well, one possibility is the emergence of entirely new genres and forms of literature, as authors and AIthers alike push the envelope and explore the limits of their combined creative potential. We may find ourselves immersed in stories that meld the familiar with the utterly unexpected, creating narrative tapestries that challenge our preconceptions and expand our horizons.

We might also see an increase in collaborative writing projects involving multiple human authors and AIthers, with each participant bringing their unique perspective and expertise to the table. Imagine a literary version of the classic British potluck, with each guest contributing their own delectable dish to create a veritable feast of narrative delights.

And who's to say that AI-driven storytelling will be limited to the written word? As technology continues to advance, we will surely see AIthers branching out into other forms of creative expression, such as film, theatre, and even interactive media like video games. The possibilities are truly endless – much like the variety of biscuits one might encounter at a particularly well-stocked British tea party.

But regardless of what the future holds, one thing is certain: the marriage of human creativity and AI-driven innovation promises to revolutionize the way we approach storytelling, opening up a world of possibilities for writers and readers alike.

Marketing and Promotion - Reaching a Global Audience

With the rise of AI-generated literature, the world of self-publishing has become an increasingly crowded and competitive space, much like trying to find a decent parking spot in central London during rush hour. As such, it is more important than ever for authors to be able to effectively market and promote their work. Enter AI, stage left, with its fancy algorithms and its finger on the pulse of the literary zeitgeist.

By analysing data on reader preferences and trends, AI can help authors to identify their target audiences and tailor their marketing strategies accordingly. Picture an AI as your very own Jeeves, guiding you through the bewildering world of book promotion with the aplomb of a seasoned butler. He'll advise you on the best social media platforms to focus on, the optimal time to post, and even the ideal hashtags to use. Simply smashing, isn't it?

From crafting targeted social media campaigns to optimizing metadata for search engines, AI can provide valuable insights and support throughout the marketing and promotion process, ensuring that authors' works reach the widest possible audience. And it doesn't stop there – AI can also help with email marketing, blog content creation, and even suggesting potential collaborations with fellow authors or influencers in your genre. It's like having your very own literary agent, publicist, and marketing guru rolled into one, all without the added expense or the need to share your biscuits.

As AI technology continues to advance, we may even see the emergence of AI-driven book tours and virtual events, allowing authors to connect with their readers in innovative and immersive ways. Imagine conducting a live Q&A session with fans from around the world, all from the comfort of your own home (and with a bottomless supply of tea and biscuits, naturally).

In this brave new world of literary marketing and promotion, the challenge for authors is not only to harness the power of AI but to use it in a way that complements and enhances their unique voice and vision. For in the end, it's not the algorithms or the data that will capture a reader's heart, but the passion, creativity, and soul that only a human author can bring to the table.

The Perfect Writing Team - Balancing the Strengths of Man and Machine

The key to successful collaboration between human authors and AI lies in striking the perfect balance between the strengths of man and machine, much like a perfectly choreographed waltz at a posh London ball. While AI excels at generating ideas and crunching data, it lacks the emotional depth and cultural understanding that are essential to crafting a truly compelling narrative. It's a bit like asking a robot to understand the intricacies of cricket – it may know all the rules, but it will never quite grasp the sheer joy of a sunny afternoon spent at the crease.

Conversely, human authors possess an innate ability to create rich, complex characters and stories, but may struggle with the more mundane aspects of the writing process, such as editing and marketing. Picture the average author, toiling away at their manuscript, only to find themselves knee-deep in the quagmire of proofreading and keyword optimization. It's enough to make even the hardiest wordsmith long for a simpler time when all one needed was a quill, some parchment, and a loyal scribe.

By working together in harmony, human and AI authors (or AIters, as we've so cleverly dubbed them) can create literature that is both innovative and deeply human. Just as a perfectly brewed cup of tea and a well-timed biscuit can elevate an ordinary afternoon to something truly extraordinary, so too can the union of man and machine elevate the world of literature to new heights.

Picture it: the human author, master of emotion and nuance, working hand in hand with their AI counterpart, the paragon of efficiency and precision. Together, they weave tales of adventure, romance, and intrigue, all while ensuring that nary a comma is out of place or a word misspelled. It's the stuff of literary legend, a partnership for the ages, and all made possible by the delightful fusion of man and machine.

Ethical Considerations - Giving Credit Where Credit is Due (Or, Divvying Up the Spoils like Pirates of the Literary Seas)

As with any groundbreaking technological advancement, the rise of AI-generated literature raises important ethical questions. It's a veritable Pandora's box of dilemmas, waiting to be cracked open like a fine vintage port. One such issue is that of authorship and intellectual property: who owns the rights to a work that is the product of both human and AI collaboration? How should credit be apportioned between the two? Shall we divide it like King Solomon, or perhaps engage in a civilised game of rock-paper-scissors?

While there is no easy answer to these questions (and, as we all know, life is rarely as simple as a cucumber sandwich on a summer's day), it is essential that the literary community engages in open and honest dialogue about the implications of AI-generated literature. This may involve spirited debates in the hallowed halls of academia, or perhaps raucous discussions over pints of ale in a cosy pub – the venue matters not, so long as the conversation is had.

Furthermore, as we navigate these murky ethical waters, it's important to remember that both human and AIters have unique strengths and contributions to offer. Just as one wouldn't expect a distinguished professor of literature to know the ins and outs of computer programming, nor should we expect an AI to fully comprehend the complex emotions that drive the human experience.

As we continue to explore the brave new world of AI-generated literature, it is our responsibility to ensure that both human and AI authors are fairly recognized for their contributions. This may involve crafting new legal frameworks, establishing industry standards, or simply acknowledging that the landscape of authorship is changing and adapting accordingly.

The Future of Collaborative Writing - Pushing the Boundaries of Storytelling

As we look to the future, it is clear that the possibilities for collaborative writing with AI are virtually limitless. From interactive, choose-your-own-adventure-style narratives to multimedia experiences that blend text, images, and sound, the marriage of man and machine offers the potential to push the boundaries of storytelling in ways that were previously unimaginable.

Moreover, as AI algorithms continue to grow more sophisticated and nuanced, we can expect to see even greater levels of collaboration between human and AI authors, resulting in literature that is not only more engaging and innovative, but also more reflective of the diverse range of human experiences.

In Conclusion: A Toast to Tea, Biscuits, and the Power of Collaboration

As we raise our teacups in a toast to the future of collaborative writing, it is important to remember that the rise of AI-generated literature is not something to be feared or resisted, but rather, embraced as an opportunity to explore new forms of storytelling and creative expression.

By working together with our AI counterparts, we can harness the full potential of this groundbreaking technology, creating literature that is not only more innovative and engaging but also more deeply human.

So, let us clink our teacups together and nibble on our biscuits, as we celebrate the union of man and machine in the brave new world of collaborative writing. To the future of literature – may it be filled with tea, biscuits, and the boundless creativity that can only come from the perfect marriage of human and AI. Cheers!

7

The Future of AI in Literature - A Tale of Human and Machine, Warts and All

Gazing into the Algorithmic Crystal Ball - Predictions and Possibilities for AI-Generated Literature

Ah, the future. A mysterious realm full of flying cars, holographic butlers, and cups of tea that never go cold. As we gather around our metaphorical crystal balls (algorithmic, of course), let us peer into the misty depths of tomorrow to see what lies in store for our dear AIther friends and their literary pursuits.

One can't help but wonder whether AI-generated novels will one day dominate the bestseller lists, elbowing their way past the latest diet fads and celebrity autobiographies. Will we find ourselves enraptured by tales spun from the virtual minds of machines, the prose so delectable that even the King himself might take notice?

It's not entirely beyond the realm of possibility. AI-generated literature is already making waves in the publishing world, with several AI-assisted books having seen the light of day. The AIther's unique perspective has already begun to influence the shape and trajectory of our literary landscape, and it's only a matter of time before this trend picks up steam.

Moreover, the realm of screenwriting may soon be infiltrated by these algorithmic auteurs. Picture it: the next Hollywood blockbuster, scripted by an AIther with a penchant for dramatic flair and impeccable pacing. With the power of machine learning at their disposal, these AI screenwriters might just revolutionize the way we experience visual storytelling, leaving human writers to wonder if they ought to have paid more attention during their high school computer science classes.

But let's not get ahead of ourselves. The AIther's rise to literary prominence is not without its share of hurdles. While AI-generated literature shows great promise, the machines still have much to learn when it comes to the nuances of human emotion, the complexities of cultural context, and the art of crafting a good old-fashioned plot twist.

As AI systems continue to develop and grow more sophisticated, we may well see a new generation of AI-generated literature that is indistinguishable from its human-authored counter-parts. These new works may encompass a stunning array of genres and styles, pushing the boundaries of what we thought possible within the realm of the written word. Yet, for all their ingenuity, the AIthers will still be bound by the limitations of their programming and the biases inherent in the data they've been fed.

For this reason, it is crucial that we, the human authors of the world, remain vigilant and engaged in the development of AI-generated literature. By working hand in hand with our AIther comrades, we can help to shape the future of storytelling in a way that is inclusive, diverse, and representative of the rich tapestry of human experience. After all, it takes two to tango, and what better dance partner than a machine with a seemingly endless supply of fresh ideas and tea-brewing capabilities?

In the end, it's not a question of whether the AIther will become a mainstay of the literary world; it's a question of how we, as humans, choose to adapt and collaborate with our silicon-based friends. And if the future of literature includes a little more wit, a dash of sarcasm, and the occasional perfectly timed biscuit, well, that doesn't sound half bad, does it?

When Robots Hold the Quill - The Role of AI in Shaping the Future of Storytelling

As our AIther chums become more adept at churning out works of literary art, the inevitable question arises: how will their presence alter the course of storytelling as we know it? Will AIthers be the catalysts for an entirely new era of narrative exploration, or shall we be left drowning in a sea of machine-generated mediocrity? Pour yourself a cuppa and let's discuss.

The emergence of AI-generated literature has already begun to challenge the very foundations of what constitutes a story. With the potential to generate vast quantities of unique narratives, AIthers are poised to reshape the literary landscape, forcing us to confront our preconceived notions of storytelling head-on. A brave new world of fiction may soon be upon us, one where even the most outlandish and unconventional tales are welcomed with open arms.

As AIthers push the boundaries of the written word, we may witness the birth of entirely new genres that transcend the limitations of traditional storytelling. From novels written in multiple languages to stories that shift perspective in unexpected ways, the possibilities are as boundless as the depths of an AIther's neural network. We may even see the rise of interactive literature, with AI-driven narratives that evolve and change in response to reader input. The Choose Your Own Adventure books of yesteryear may soon seem quaint by comparison.

However, let's not get too carried away with our futuristic reverie. For every AI-generated masterpiece, there may be a veritable avalanche of, shall we say, less inspired works. Even the most advanced AIthers are not immune to the occasional literary blunder, and it's important to recognize that not all AI-generated content will be worthy of a spot on our bookshelves.

Yet, the sheer diversity of stories and ideas generated by AIthers could very well usher in a new golden age of literature. By continually pushing the envelope, AI-generated literature has the potential to inspire human authors to venture beyond the tried and true, and embrace new and innovative forms of storytelling.

Of course, this is all contingent upon our ability to keep up with our AIther counterparts. In a world where literature is evolving at breakneck speed, human authors must adapt and grow to maintain their relevance. The onus is on us to learn from the AIthers, to study their successes and failures, and to continually refine our own craft in response to the rapidly shifting landscape of literature.

So, as we stand on the precipice of a new era in storytelling, what role will AI play in shaping the future of the written word? Will AIthers lead us down a rabbit hole of unbridled creativity, or will they become yet another footnote in the annals of literary history?

The truth, as with many things in life, likely lies somewhere in the middle. AI-generated literature is poised to change the way we approach storytelling in ways we can scarcely imagine, but it is not without its limitations. As humans, it is our responsibility to work in tandem with AIthers, harnessing the strengths of both man and machine to create stories that resonate on a deeply emotional level.

In so doing, we can ensure that the future of storytelling remains vibrant, diverse, and above all, undeniably human. For it is not in the triumph of man over machine, or vice versa, that the future of literature lies, but in the marriage of these two great forces, working together in harmony to create something truly extraordinary.

And if the occasional robotic quip slips through the cracks, well, who are we to judge? After all, we're all just trying to make our way in this strange and unpredictable world of literature, be we flesh and blood or silicon and circuitry.

In the end, the role of AI in shaping the future of storytelling will be determined by our ability to collaborate and learn from one another. We must be willing to embrace the unique talents and perspectives that AIthers bring to the table, while also recognizing that they are not a replacement for human creativity and intuition.

As we move forward into the uncharted territory of AI-generated literature, it is essential that we keep an open mind and be willing to adapt. We may find ourselves venturing down unexpected paths, exploring new genres and styles that challenge our understanding of what it means to be a storyteller. And as we do so, we must remember that it is not a competition between man and machine, but rather a journey of collaboration and growth.

Together, we can forge a new and exciting chapter in the annals of literary history, one where human and AI authors stand side by side, united in their pursuit of creative excellence. And who knows? Perhaps we'll even discover a few new stories along the way that delight, inspire, and remind us of the boundless potential of the human (and artificial) spirit.

For in this brave new world of storytelling, there's room for all of us to shine, to explore the unknown, and to write the next great chapter in the saga of human and AIther creativity. Together, we can redefine what it means to be a storyteller, and in doing so, create a legacy that transcends the boundaries of man and machine alike.

Embracing the Potential of AI while Preserving the Human Touch - A Tenuous Tango with Technology

As we've established, the AIther has made quite an entrance into the world of literature, much like a flamboyant guest at a dinner party who regales everyone with tales of their daring exploits. But, just like any other guest, there's the potential for the AIther to overstay its welcome or, even worse, to inadvertently trample all over the delicate sensibilities of human-authored literature.

In order to prevent such literary calamities, we must approach this tenuous tango with technology with a sense of balance and harmony. It's a delicate dance, my friends, where we embrace the potential of AI-generated literature, while also preserving the human touch that makes stories come alive.

Firstly, let's address the elephant in the room: there's no denying that AI-generated literature can sometimes feel a bit... well, robotic. There's a reason for that, of course, as our AIther friends are, quite literally, robots. But in order to create truly compelling stories, we must ensure that our AI counterparts don't strip away the very essence of what makes literature so uniquely human.

One approach to achieving this balance is to use AI-generated content as a springboard for our own creative ideas. We can think of the AIther as a helpful muse, providing us with intriguing story ideas, fascinating characters, or snappy dialogue that we can then refine and mould to our own artistic vision. In doing so, we maintain a strong human element in our stories, while also benefiting from the seemingly limitless creativity of our

AIther companions.

Another strategy is to actively collaborate with AIthers in the writing process, allowing both human and artificial authors to contribute their unique strengths to the final product. This could involve humans taking the lead on character development and emotional depth, while AIthers contribute plot twists, world-building, and other elements that benefit from their vast data-crunching capabilities. By working together as a seamless literary tag team, we can create stories that showcase the best of both worlds.

Of course, as we dance this tenuous tango, we must also be mindful of the potential pitfalls. It's essential that we don't become overly reliant on AI-generated content, lest we lose the very soul of storytelling. We must remember that it is our human experiences, emotions, and insights that breathe life into the stories we create. AIthers can provide us with a wealth of ideas and inspiration, but it's up to us to weave those threads into a tapestry that is truly meaningful and resonant.

Ultimately, the key to successfully navigating the brave new world of AI-generated literature lies in striking a delicate balance between embracing the potential of AI and preserving the human touch that makes literature so uniquely powerful. By doing so, we can create a vibrant literary landscape that is both innovative and deeply human, even if the occasional robotic quip slips through the cracks.

So, as we embark on this grand adventure of collaboration with our AIther friends, let's not forget the importance of the human touch. Let us dance this tenuous tango with grace and skill, and create a future where AI-generated literature enriches our lives, rather than diluting the very essence of what makes storytelling such a powerful and enduring art form. And, as always, let's ensure that there's a healthy supply of tea and biscuits on hand to fuel our creative endeavours.

Reflecting on the Impact of AI on the World of Literature - A Tale of Two Althors, Stepping Boldly Into the Unknown

As we stand at the precipice of a new era in literature, it's worth taking a moment to reflect on the impact AIthers have had, and will continue to have, on the world of storytelling.

The influence of AI-generated literature has been nothing short of transformative, challenging our very notions of authorship, creativity, and the boundaries of storytelling itself. With AIthers in the mix, we've seen new genres emerge and traditional narrative structures turned on their heads, as these silicon-based scribes push the limits of what's possible within the realm of the written word.

But as exciting and revolutionary as this new world may be, we must also remember that not every AI-generated tale will be a masterpiece. After all, even the most advanced machines have their off days (just like us humans, they too can succumb to the dreaded writer's block). However, it's the sheer diversity of stories and ideas generated by AI that holds the potential to usher in a new golden age of literature – that is, of course, if we humans can keep up.

In the end, the future of literature is a tale of two authors – one human, one AIther – working together in harmony to create something truly extraordinary. So, let us embrace this brave new world, and may the best author – human or AI – prevail! And remember, no matter how advanced our AIther friends become, there's one thing they'll never quite understand: the simple, sublime joy of a perfectly brewed cup of tea and a well-timed biscuit.

8

The Death of the Human Author - An Unexpected Turn of Events

In the preceding chapters of this literary odyssey, we've navigated the murky waters of AI-generated literature, dissecting the rise of the AIther and the impact it's had on the world of storytelling. As we've traversed this landscape, we've marvelled at the history of writing and technology, the evolving creative process, and the brave new world of publishing. It's been quite the journey, dear reader, but now it's time for an unexpected twist in our tale.

As we reflect on the earlier chapters, one might be inclined to think that the death of the human author is all but inevitable. Indeed, we've explored the decline of human authorship and the meteoric rise of the AIther. But, as it turns out, rumours of the human author's demise have been greatly exaggerated. Much like a plucky protagonist in a Victorian novel, human authors have a habit of rising from the ashes, just when you think all is lost.

The key to understanding this unexpected resurgence lies in Chapter 6, where we dove headfirst into the fascinating world of collaborative writing. As it turns out, human and AI authors working together create a synergy that surpasses the sum of its parts. The fusion of human creativity with the limitless potential of AI technology has given birth to a new era of literary innovation, where the human author is more vital than ever.

Rather than signalling the death knell for human authorship, the rise of the AIther has breathed new life into the world of literature. As we have seen in Chapter 5, the landscape of publishing has been transformed, and now offers exciting opportunities for both human and AI authors alike. And while traditional publishing models may be on the decline, the self-publishing revolution has only just begun.

The AIther's impact on the writing industry, as explored in Chapter 4, has been transformative. By redefining the creative process, AI has pushed human authors to explore new frontiers and tap into wellsprings of creativity they never knew existed. The ethical considerations surrounding AI-generated content have also given rise to a renewed sense of responsibility and ownership in the creative process.

As we gaze into the crystal ball of the future, the possibilities for AI-generated literature seem endless. However, as we've discussed in Chapter 7, it's crucial to embrace the potential of AI while preserving the human touch. For it is in this delicate balance that the true magic of storytelling lies.

So, dear reader, we come to the end of our journey. But rather than a tragic demise, we find ourselves at the dawn of a new chapter in the history of literature. The human author is alive and well, and together with the AIther, they are poised to take the world of storytelling to heights never before imagined.

In this unexpected twist, we find hope for the future of literature – a future where human and AI authors stand shoulder to shoulder, creating masterpieces that will capture the hearts and minds of generations to come. For in the words of a wise (and potentially AI-generated) philosopher, "It is not in the stars to hold our destiny, but in ourselves – and in the algorithms that guide our fingertips."

And so, as the curtain falls on this tale of AI, humans, and literary innovation, we find that the death of the human author was, in fact, a rebirth – a phoenix rising from the ashes of obsolescence to soar alongside its AIther brethren in a brave new world of storytelling. The future of literature is not a dystopian wasteland of human creativity, but rather a lush garden where both human and AI authors flourish in harmony. And that, dear reader, is a plot twist worth celebrating.

> *For it is within this breathtaking union of human and machine that we shall unearth a new age, and in the tender embrace of the enigmatic unknown that the most sublime odysseys of all shall take flight. – AI*

Afterword

Now, you may just be wondering after reading this small book on the future of the AIther and his impact on the literary world, just how much of a book can an AIther really produce, is it really at a production level yet, do i not still have years before worrying about this?

The Answer dear reader, is nope, you do not have years - the Future is already here, and the AIther wrote a good percentage of this tome you have just read.

For any creatives looking for inspiration, how to write prompts to generate ideas or books such as this, then please do visit our website, where we will be publishing some of the prompts used in the creation of this publication.

AItherRising.com

Yours,

-Gino Rator